Emily Jupp

Wormholes

Salamander Street

PLAYS

First published in 2024 by Salamander Street Ltd., a Wordville imprint. (info@salamanderstreetcom).

Wormholes © Emily Jupp, 2024

All rights reserved.

Cover Photography: Harry Livingstone

PB ISBN: 9781068696206

10 9 8 7 6 5 4 3 2 1

Further copies of this publication can be purchased from www.salamanderstreet.com

Wordville

INTRODUCTION

Wormholes was inspired by a string of relationships in my 20s, which were manipulative, controlling or just downright horrible. I wanted to write something that detailed those relationships and the corrosive effect it would have had if I had stayed in them. I also didn't want the play to be a two-hander; giving both parties in the relationship equal air time. I was fed up with the narrative that there are two sides to every story, which people who haven't experienced an abusive relationship often say. I wanted to show them the slow drip-feed, the insidiousness of it. It was important to me that the woman at the heart of the story was a confident, strong woman, as we often are—and I also wanted her to be an Everywoman, because abuse doesn't descriminate on grounds of race, class, wealth, geography or any other identifying factor, except that mostly, men are the perpetrators.

There was a recent meme that asked women if they would rather be lost in a forest with a bear or a man—and most women chose the bear. We are living at a time when women feel scared. According to helpline data, domestic abuse has only risen in the last couple of years—and half of female victims of lethal violence in this country die at the hands of a man they know—in the home. At least one in four women experiences domestic abuse. This is not a rare issue, it is everywhere and it's on the rise.

While the statistics are there for anyone to read, I've found through discussions about the play that there is still a gap in understanding how common this is and what the signs are. I'm hoping that showing what it's like from the inside will help people to empathise and understand it.

Emily Jupp
2024

ACKNOWLEDGEMENTS

I'd like to thank my Mum and Dad. Mum especially for teaching me to read when she realised my teachers weren't doing a great job of it. I've been a lover of words ever since. Thanks to Jamie for being supportive, coming to at least three nights and not complaining about it and managing to convince members of the Metroplitan Police to come and see it too. Thanks to Victoria for being one of the best actors on the planet and for saying yes from the get-go. Your talent astounds me. Thanks to Scott for really getting it, for his nuance and empathy—and thanks to Kev for letting me talk it out when self-producing a play got a bit much. Thank you to the amazing creative team who have brought these words to life. You all make magic happen. The fact you are still making magic happen after a decade of Tory rule and the relentless erosion of our creative industries is an actual miracle. Let's hope better days are coming very soon.

I can't praise the wonderful women of Refuge enough. Becks Bond and Idu Nwokolo have supported the journey of *Wormholes* for the past year. Idu helped me and Victoria to connect with Survivors, who are some of the most amazing people—and we would like to thank them too. I won't identify the Survivors personally here, as not all can be named for protection purposes but they know who they are and I want to thank them for opening up and trusting us with their stories—and for giving *Wormholes* their whole-hearted support. *Wormholes* is theirs too.

Thank you to Marie McCarthy, Artistic Director of the Omnibus Theatre, for immediately saying yes to the show and then for being very patient for a year and a half while we scrabbled together some funding and then for saying yes again when we barely had enough money to put it on. I'm hugely grateful. Thank you also to all of the Omnibus team, who've been cheerleading the play, especially Sam Pout whose dramaturgy skills have taken the text up by several notches in quality with his gentle suggestions.

Thank you to Chloé Nelkin Consulting for working so hard to get *Wormholes* out there; to Phoebe Cave, my hardworking account manager and to Chloé for always loving my words, whatever form they take—and for being a kind friend.

I'd also like to thank the body of work that I read and went to see as part of my research—the amazing writers in the canon of talking about the use and abuse of women, their bodies and how society sees us when it's at its worst: *Prima Facie* by Suzie Miller, *Machinal* by Sophie Treadwell, *The Chain* by Chimene Suleyman, *it felt empty when the heart went at first but it is alright now*, by Lucy Kirkwood, *Girls and Boys* by Dennis Kelly.

And of course, thanks to Lucy at Salamander Street for publishing this! It's such a special thing to have a play in print, thank you for making it happen despite the ridiculously short turnaround!

A portion of the profts from each copy of *Wormholes* sold will be donated to Refuge, a UK charity providing specialist support for women and children experiencing domestic violence.

You are not alone. If you or someone you know is experiencing domestic abuse of any kind, Refuge can support you. Visit refuge.org.uk for more information.

Wormholes received its first professional staging at the Omnibus Theatre in London on 23 July 2024, with Victoria Yeates in the role of Woman.

CAST

ALL: **Victoria Yeates**

CREATIVES

Writer: **Emily Jupp**

Director: **Scott Le Crass**

Production Manager: **Kevin Nolan**

Set and Costume Designer: **Leah Kelly**

Lighting Designer: **Jodie Underwood**

Music Designers: **Paul Housden and Gary Cansell**

Stage Manager: **Roel Fox**

Dramaturg: **Sam Pout**

ABOUT THE CAST AND CREATIVES

VICTORIA YEATES | Actor

Victoria Yeates made her Royal Shakespeare Company debut as Imogen Holst in *Ben and Imo* by Mark Ravenhill. Victoria appears as Bunty in the *Fantastic Beasts* films, *The Crimes of Grindelwald* and its sequel, *The Secrets of Dumbledore*. She is well known for playing the role of Sister Winifred in *Call The Midwife* (BBC), with other television credits including *A Discovery of Witches* (Sky). Victoria's other theatre credits include: Jean Harlow in Michael McClure's *The Beard* (Old Red Lion), *Big Love* (The Gate), *The Crucible* (Queens Theatre Hornchurch/ATG tour), *Don Juan Comes Back From The War* and *Pains of Youth* (Belgrade Theatre), *Wuthering Heights* (Birmingham Rep/tour), *Rookery Nook* (Menier Chocolate Factory), *The League of Youth, Private Lives* (Nottingham Playhouse) and *The Dogwalker* (Jermyn Street). *Wormholes* is her first solo show.

EMILY JUPP | Writer

After a long career as a national newspaper journalist, Emily branched into writing for television and stage in 2016. Her first play *Doing Well*, about the mental health crisis affecting young people and its links to social media, took a satirical swipe at the cult of influencers. It was a finalist for the Liverpool Hope Prize in 2019. *Wormholes* was longlisted for The Bruntwood Prize in 2022 under its previous title, *Funny Farm*. Emily is currently working on a screenplay with Victoria Yeates, a novel, co-writing two books and working on another play about the climate crisis and the men's rights movement.

SCOTT LE CRASS | Director

Scott's major credits include: *Jab* by James McDermott starring Kacey Ainsworth, *Cut The Crap* with Sharon Osborne, *Toxic* starring Nathaniel J Hall, *Buff* by Ben Fensome (winner of Playbill Pick of the Fringe at Edinburgh Festival 2023) and Offie-Award winning *Country Music* by Simon Stephens. Last year he was nominated for Best Creative West End Debut at The Stage Awards for *Rose* by Martin Sherman, starring Maureen Lipman.

KEVIN NOLAN | Production Manager

Kevin is a theatre and filmed media producer based in London. Theatre credits include: *Jab* (Finborough Theatre, London), *Buff* (Pleasance, Edinburgh), *A Queermas Carol* (Wheatsheaf Hall, London) and *Country Music* (Omnibus Theatre, London). Film credits include: *Queer Shame* and *We 3 Queers* (both Q&T Media).

LEAH KELLY | Stage Design

Leah is a performance designer for stage. She graduated in Fine Art at Manchester School of Art in 2023. Her credits include *Banging Denmark* (Finborough Theatre), *Jab* (Finborough Theatre) and *Costume Blood on Your Hands* (Southwark Playhouse).

JODIE UNDERWOOD | Lighting Designer

Jodie trained at RADA. Lighting credits includes: *A Christmas Carol* (Brewhouse Taunton); *Cheeky Little Brown* (UK Tour); *The Life Sporadic of Jess Wildgoose* (Pleasance London and Pleasance Edinburgh); *DNA* (Tara Theatre), *After The Act* (New Diorama Theatre and Traverse Theatre, Edinburgh); *Blow Down* (Theatre Royal Wakefield and Leeds Playhouse); *The Boys Are Kissing* (Theatre503) and *Horse-Play* (Riverside Studios). Associate Lighting Designs include: *Ruckus* (UK Tour); *The Book Of Will* (Shakespeare North Playhouse); *Ride* (Leicester Curve and Southwark Playhouse); *Pigs Might Fly* (Theatre Peckham) and *When Darkness Falls* (UK Tour).

PAUL HOUSDEN | Sound Designer & Composer

Paul Housden is an Australian multi-instrumentalist composer and singer based in London. He honed his eclectic production and musical skills over many years as a self-produced solo artist and frontman of psych band *Gentlemen*. In 2010, Paul scored his first short *Muscles* directed by his brother Edward Housden, which received official selection at Cannes. Other short scores include *Homebodies* (Best Narrative Short Nominee, 2016), *Playpals* (2018) by Yianni Warnock, and *Multiplex* (2020) by Jed Shepherd. He also composed the themes for ITV2 shows *2Awesome* and *Dating In The Dark*. Recently Paul scored an acclaimed podcast/documentary series called *The Super Hero Complex* for iHeartMedia.

ROEL FOX | Stage Manager

Roel Fox is an Amsterdam-born Tech Operator, Stage-Manager, Actor-Musician, Composer, Assistant-Director, Music Director and Singing Teacher. His Operator and Stage Manager credits across London Fringe Theatre venues include: South Kentish Town (Arcola), *Improbotics: Rosetta Stone* (Rich Mix), *Pool No Water, Fury, 4:48 Psychosis* (Drayton Arms), *Don Juan Comes Back From The War* (The New Diorama), *Wild East* (Theatre 503), *Buff* (The Vaults), *Behold! The Monkey Jesus* (The Brockley Jack), and *Jab* (Finborough Theatre). Some of his stage credits include: *Vikings at Helgeland* (Drayton Arms), *The Accidental Death Of An Anarchist* (OSO Arts Centre), Hamlet (Tang Xianzu Theatre), and *Epic Love* and *Pop Songs* (New Wimbledon Theatre).

SAM POUT | Dramaturg

Sam is a playwright and dramaturg and is Literary Associate at Omnibus Theatre.

His dramaturgy includes: *Scarlet Sunday* (2024), *Compositor E* (2023), *The Woman Who Turned into a Tree* (2023), *Merboy* (2023) and *Drum* (2022) (Omnibus Theatre) *Drum* (New Diorama Theatre/Edinburgh Festival Fringe, 2024) and *Rapture* (Pleasance Theatre, 2022). Sam has also worked on the development of plays leading to professional production at Soho Theatre, VAULT Festival and Theatre 503. His playwriting includes *Fisheye* (Omnibus Theatre, 2023) and *The Brave Anthology* which he also directed (Edinburgh Festival Fringe, 2019). Sam studied BA Drama and Theatre studies at Royal Holloway, University of London and has an MA in Dramaturgy and Writing for Performance at Goldsmiths, University of London.

Emily Jupp

Wormholes

CHARACTERS

WOMAN

Late-thirties

NOTES ON THE PLAY

This was first performed as a one-actor play, with Victoria Yeates reading all the parts. It could be adapted to include a larger cast that would include Woman's Mother, her friend Jess—and Him.

Information in (brackets) is used to add clarity and context about what WOMAN is thinking, her gestures and who is speaking to her. You may choose for her to speak the thoughts out loud, or keep them to herself. A dash— is an unfinished sentence or thought.

This script represents the play at the time of rehearsal and there could be changes during the production.

SCENE ONE

WOMAN is in a bright, halogen-lit, white-walled room. Sometimes, there is soil. Snoring sound.

WOMAN: I like it here. It's very... calm. Even the nutters. Mary —she's in the room next to mine and I never hear a peep out of her. Sometimes she'll sidle up to me during a yoga class or something and she'll whisper: 'I'm not really supposed to be here.'

That's when you know, when someone tells you that, they really, really are meant to be here. Mary's alright though, just talks to people who aren't there sometimes. And she likes to play a game where she convinces the newbies that she's in charge. Harmless though.

I just keep my head down. It's safer that way. I need those blinkers that horses have, you know, to keep them from getting scared.

There's a sound like a tape recorder being pressed on and a dim whirring.

How'd I get here? Took a bus.

Pause.

Ha! Yeah, I know what you mean. (*Loud, flicker of anger*) It's a bit personal isn't it? (*Then calm again*) We don't really know each other. How'd you *two* get here?

Listens to reply.

Hmm. That's what they all say.

MARY pokes her head round the door.

Oops, sorry Mary, we're using this room. (*Humouring her*) Nope I can't understand it either, they've got it all mixed up, yeah, topsy turvy!

(*Addressing questioners, conspiratorially*) That's Mary. (*Makes loopy sign*) What are you looking at me like that for?

Where was I?—yeah. How I got here.

You know, the world's getting better. We've got a lot to be happy about. Our lives are incredibly comfortable. Our grandparents had to go to wars and piss in a loo in their garden. My grandma was one of ten, born in a slum in Kings Cross. That wasn't that long ago... Look at us now! Slum-free! With inside loos! Think about genome sequencing! The swift roll-out of the vaccines. Extreme poverty is falling (what about the cost of living?) Ninety per cent of the world has electricity now (don't think about the ten per cent). The gender pay gap is closing... very slowly. Guinea Worm has nearly been eradicated. Which is a *good thing*, but as I didn't know about it until I googled 'ways the world is getting better', it's also kind of a *bad* thing? because now (*increasingly serious*) just before I fall asleep...

Beat.

...I think about being in the 0.00000000001 per cent of people who contract Guinea Worm. Do you know the symptoms of Guinea Worm? I've googled them. The worm comes into a human body where it lives for a year, undetected, getting nice and fat and long—like, a metre long. But the funny thing is, you don't notice it. It happens so slowly. It starts off like a tiny, harmless larva, just a bud of a thing. But then it grows, taking up space, space inside you, and you still don't see it for what it is; you carry on your life, just slightly impaired, an ache there, a sting here—but you're managing. No-one looking at you would spot a thing out of place. You're complacent. You and the worm coexist, even though it's eating you from the inside, you've got no idea.

But the world is getting better (*like a mantra to self*), the world is getting better. Microchips are really small now... (*thinks hard*) Bees! Think of the bees! They're great. They'll save us from this internet-powered ballet of doom.

Pause.

Friends? In here? Not really. None from outside either. Not because I went—(although that probably didn't help). They all left before that... Fuck 'em. With friends like that! But then. You start to question things, in here. *You lot (with a vague gesture to one of the questioners)* call it 'growth'. I call it bloody hard work.

You start going over things. Retracing your steps. You start questioning what you thought was reality—and suspect there was another, alternative reality, lurking underneath. Like parallel dimensions. Like wormholes.

So yeah. I had friends before. Close friends. When we all got together, we used to talk for hours and not stop for breath. My ride or dies. I can hear them now.

Anna, a goth, but a happy one. Merrily pansexual, always carries a giant backpack, but no-one knows what's in it.

Shadé—married in her 20s, two kids by 27, CEO by 30. Wildly efficient, terrifyingly smart. Doesn't hate her husband, but sees him as increasingly irrelevant.

Then there's Jess. My Jess. The rest of us met at uni but I've known Jess since school. I know her so well it's hard to describe her, like describing a part of yourself. She's just fun. We giggle. We talk about her boyfriends, she always gets so caught up with each one, even though they are soooo wrong for her. Be like me, I say, care a bit less. There will always be men, they're half the population. They're not bloody going anywhere! But she won't listen. She has these sudden wild obsessions. She thinks each new date could be 'The one'! I'm... not so quick to invest. I usually get to three dates, three fun dates, before the conversation dries up and my calendar gets too busy and we drift our separate ways. Jess is in such a rush. She treats dating like a job hunt, with interviews and CVs, she can't enjoy hanging out with a member of the opposite sex without fantasising about baby names. It's probably not good for her to spend so much energy on these men, but it does make for some very entertaining stories.

We meet for lunch. Our offices are close enough we can meet in the middle in ten minutes. I do accounts at a big data company. No idea what they actually do. Don't care. She's in advertising.

She starts off with 'You know how my religion is really important to me?' I don't. It isn't. I nod. 'So I saw this stunning man on my way to the station last week and I just knew we had a connection, so I followed him and he went into this church and so I decided I'd go too and then we got talking and he was like, 'are you new here?' and I was like, 'yeah'. Isn't that great! He noticed me! I just know he knows we're meant to be. So I'm volunteering there this Saturday at the soup kitchen so that's basically a date isn't it?'

'Er... no.'

'OK, maybe you weren't listening properly, 'cos it definitely is.'

'Or... on the other hand... maybe you're stalking him?'

'I don't know why you're being so negative when this could be my one - (*sob*) my one... my one chance at love!'

'Oh! I'm sorry, yeah I get it now. Of course. It's meant to be. Be careful though, don't get your heart crushed.

That's the thing about her. Her heart's always open.

Here comes Tracey. (*She acts casual*) 'Alright'?

Her eyes follow the invisible TRACEY across the room, until she exits.

Tracey. She's all sexy and bulimic. Like Angelina Jolie in 'Girl, Interrupted'. Glamorous, dangerous. Never says hello. Great fluorescent nails.

WOMAN looks at her short, ragged nails, hides them behind her back, nervously.

Look at her—you can tell she was the type to... drop everything and go dancing on a Tuesday night, rock up to work in yesterday's clothes and change in the loos. Caring though, loyal. Doesn't make friends easy but when she does...

set for life. Not now though, that's been beaten out of her. The problem with being aloof in a place like this is everyone just leaves you alone. I bet it's all a front. She must be lonely. That's why I keep trying with her. Just in case she feels like saying 'hi' back one day.

So, yeah, wormholes.

(*Shifting to a moment in the past, prompted by the questioner*) What? Him?

The first time? (*She thinks, a small cynical laugh*) It's not that simple, is it? It builds up... If he feels bad and acts a bit unreasonable, that's not... that's what everyone does from time to time, it doesn't mean... Well, I'll tell you but it's not—(*she's cut off pauses and listens*)

OK, OK. But you need the first bit. The good bit.

It's early days. We've been loved up tucked under a duvet for 36 hours straight, we only leave the bedroom to scavenge cheese and crackers and order greasy noodles from the Chinese takeaway. It is hot between us. We keep complimenting each other on how good we are at sex. He's got this thin, boyish waist and broad shoulders, which I am obsessed with. I'm not keen on his stupid 90s throwback haircut. It's always flopping around in his eyes and at first I thought it was because he genuinely did not care about how he looked, but then I realised it was carefully constructed to make him look as though he didn't care. Which is a bit different, isn't it?

I dunno if he's Mr Right, we've not had much conversation to judge. But that kind of sex, it has to mean something, doesn't it? When you feel that amazing, that connected. Honestly, it's like movie sex, it's like a drug, except there's no comedown. I'm telling you because this is important information, I'm not just, like, bragging. The world needs to know that really great sex is possible, cos I certainly didn't until him. Sex like that... It's very compelling. Very moreish. Like cocaine... or Monster Munch. Of course, anything that feels that good must have a downside, just like Monster Munch, so I'm suspicious. Must be a trick, mustn't it? I can't possibly have met someone who makes me feel this amazing without there being something wrong with them... but we start to talk a bit, to fill the time between sessions, then one day, we actually go out, like, for dinner.

He takes me to this cute pizza place near his house where the staff know him and they're all clapping him on the back and telling me how he's a great guy and then they leave us to it.

She falls silent, we are in the restaurant.

There is too long a pause.

He holds my hand across the table.

(*Rallying*) So... (*She loses her thought. The silence is deafening*)

Thanks! Er, you too. Nice to see you with clothes on for a change. Ha! Oh, God, I didn't mean. No, you know I like you with them off too.

Pause.

Oh, well, thank you very much. Yeah, I go to the gym, just round the corner? You can see it—just over past the guy walking his ferret—yeah. I started 'cos I didn't like my arms, bit self-conscious—oh, well thanks! That's nice. That's really nice.

It's not so much what he said as how he said it? He pays attention to things I say and then when we next see each other, he repeats it, but with his own thoughts attached. It's like he's listening. That's new. Makes me feel important, like he's in awe of me. And he saves me the last slice of pizza.

After that date, he turned up at the gym—just to surprise me! He was holding a banana and a coffee and even though I was sweaty and knackered, he said I was 'glowing'! Glowing!
He asks good questions. He spontaneously makes me tea. He turns up on time. It's good.
We start to make these great plans. Our future house will be somewhere round here, a little cottage, not on the main road, but not so far back that you can't walk to the station within

15 minutes, our future dog will be an Australian cattle hound called Ramekin. We'll plant Tulips in our garden—it's all nonsense 'cos we barely know each other, but it's also kind of sweet.

SCENE TWO

Before I know it, a few weeks have passed and I've been getting messages asking whether I'm still alive. I suddenly remember I have friends. So, shagged out and feelin' fine, I say I'm gonna see my friends. Take a couple of days. I go home happy.

And—

Weeeeee're out. Glad rags, cocktails, high-high heels. Bangin' tunes. I am dancing, wiggling, jiggling. The drinks are flowing, I'm with my crew and I am aliiiiive.

Her physicality transforms as she dances with abandon.

(*She sings*) I'm every woman it's all in meeeeeee!

Then, suddenly, he's there. It's a bit strange 'cos it was meant to be girls night? but then they all just showed up, OK fine, but—

TUNE! I love this one!

WOMAN is pulled by imaginary hands onto the dancefloor and starts dancing with enthusiasm.

I love these ladies. When I'm with them, I don't want to be anywhere else.

We've got our bags on the floor and we're dancing around in a tight circle, but he keeps coming over. We haven't been dating that long, so it's hard, you know, to say, like, fuck off. I mean, we have spent all week together, and I made it clear, so I'm a bit annoyed that he's even here. But I also fancy the pants off him, so it's difficult isn't it?

He starts grinding up behind me. I try to ignore him, but that doesn't work.

My friend Jess whispers in my ear—'This your new fella, or some random?'

'Random'. I say. I'm not ready for them to meet him. I'm not even sure how I feel about him. It's just been a blur of sex. Really sexy sex. That's not enough—I could get bored soon. He might open his mouth one day and say something that just kills it. He's really hot though. But no. I didn't invite him here! He's not getting to meet them. He needs to earn it.

He keeps edging around me, like a lost dog... Why are you here?

Beat.

Coincidence?! Of all the clubs in all of town you stride into mine?!

Beat.

Of course I still wanna be with you. It's not about that. No I'm not—

He storms off and I think he's misunderstood what I've said to him. I've hurt his feelings, so I go after—he's standing by the exit, stressed and upset. I feel like something has grabbed into my stomach and twisted.

He says, if I think there's even a chance I could love him, then I should leave with him, now. He's all anguished and desperate. I realise he really cares about me. It's more than shagging, apparently. I don't understand why he needs me right now... but the girls won't mind if I leave. They've all got each other, haven't they? They don't need me there. But he clearly does. Look at him, he's a mess. Just between us, I like it. I send Jess a hasty text—'Soz felt sick gon home' and collect our coats.

I take him by the hand. Outside, we find a bench to sit on, the wind from the Thames blows up around us and we huddle closer. It's the first time he isn't being strong—he's vulnerable.

He tells me about when his dad left when he was five—went and made a whole new family over in New Zealand, he was abandoned. He felt triggered—I guess, seeing me independent and happy—even though he loves that about me—he says that's attractive... He's all soft and confused about it.

I'm here. Just breathe! breathe. It's OK, it's OK.

If I'm honest, I'm flattered I can make someone feel like that, like my actions mean so much they can make someone into a bit of a wreck! I have that power.

He's shivering, so I wrap my feather boa round his neck. He looks like a sad little parrot.

When we get home, we have sex and it feels... connected, you know, meaningful. He hugs me really tight and I think, maybe this could be the guy for me. He holds my face in his hands, tenderly, gently, kissing me, then he stares into my eyes and says; you're so fragile, I feel like I could accidentally crush you.

SCENE THREE

We come back to the present.

WOMAN is asked another question but ignores it, deflecting.

There's a little wood outside—and I'm allowed now to, like, go to the shops and stuff. Mary isn't. And when I walk through the woods on my own, to the shops, I feel free, like, I dunno, like, I am part of the earth, part of the trees. I am soil. None of my decisions are good or bad, none of it matters in the bigger, larger scheme of things. I'm just a tiny flake of dandruff on the colossal, throbbing head of existence. (Need to buy shampoo).

There's this woman in here. Leslie. You'll meet her if you stay for dinner.

Pause, the questioner responds in the negative.

Well, your loss, it's toad in the hole and ice cream for pud. So Leslie, she dresses in these amazing suits. Most people round here just wear athleisure. I used to think it was called 'ass-leisure'? Why would anyone wear sportswear to lounge around in? I didn't get it, until I came here. Now I totally do. It's like basically saying to the world I could be exercising right now. I'm not; I'm actually sitting in a comfy chair eating jaffa cakes, but I could be. Any second now, I could leap into action.

I bet you think people don't get competitive in here, but Leslie and her suits, that's like she's telling us; I'm different from you, I'm better. Work-obsessed, she is. When she first arrived here, she was midway through a work call, they had to sedate her in order to prise the phone out of her hand.

Leslie's alright. She grew up near me, actually. She's had this amazing career, been flown all over the world, business class, wining and dining with clients, got a flat in Chelsea now.

She listens.

Dunno. Something with money? She gets chatty in the evenings and she tells us about her lovers! Never been married, never had kids and loves it that way. When the other women talk about their kids she, like, sighs very loudly and when they're out of earshot she refers to their children as 'encumbrances'. A life without encumbrances. (*Enviously*) What must that be like? Do you think she's really happy? I think she is, she loves her work too much; burnout, that's why she's here. I'd rather have burnout, given a choice.

I get to use my phone here. I don't call anyone. I just keep googling, going into the little wormholes in the abyss of the internet. I keep coming back to that page about Guinea Worm. Once it gets to a certain size, once it's taken over, you find yourself feeling listless, you're tired and in pain, you might not be able to do the things you used to be able to do. The worm is stopping you. But you don't know it's the worm. You think you're just getting old. Maybe you're dying.

A question.

The Prime minister? Easy. That bigoted tosser. No. The one after the erratic hay bale. The one who doesn't ever move his arms.

(*Drifts and seems lost again*) I'm not good with names. Sorry.

Pause.

Do we have to do this? I mean going through it all, in order, like this? Can't I just sign something saying yes I am totally bat shit crazy and be done with it?

What's it got to do with Freddy? He can't hurt Fred, not where he is.

Pause.

I don't see how but—

Pause.

Alright, alright!

A year later... I'm engaged! Me! I'm living the fairytale. I see my friends' envy. That's nice, isn't it? Validating. I think Jess'll take it badly. She's the one who has dreamed about her wedding day since she was a kid. I worry she'll think I don't deserve it, cos she's put all the effort in, so why me and not her? But she's amazing. She's so happy for me. She asks me about stuff that I didn't know you had to think about, like playlists and colour schemes and cake. Jess and I do a lot of cake testing. I start to see what all the fuss is about and I get excited. We look at venues and catering, Jess and I... I get a picture in my head of the day and it's just perfect.

I made a Pinterest board! Look at these flowers! No? Well, they're peonies. They are a bit expensive but it's our wedding babe! We'll only do it once! OK, alright, just my bouquet. I guess the venue is pretty enough without extra flowers. Yeah, it would be OTT, wouldn't it...? I probably got a bit carried away with Jess. I found the dream dress though! Well, it's got handmade lace—I—

Well it is classic, lace is classic! What if I pay? It's not emasculating! I pay for all my other dresses, why not this one?

What if we take the best man's suit off the budget and we trim down the choice of main... there! Then we can afford my dress!

I'm not trying to show you up...

It goes on, for hours, until I'm just tired of it. I'm done, I'm out. It was nice to imagine it all with Jess, but I probably got carried away with her ideas. Better to save the money for a rainy day.

I tell my mates we want an intimate, exclusive feel. They look at me; you've changed. I nod, oh yes. Look at me, I'm mature now, I understand that relationships are about hard work and compromise. Compromise. I keep compromising. I'm very good at it.

We don't need a big wedding, do we? We just need each other, a couple of witnesses, modest registry office do. That's best, best for both of us.

It's only one day. It doesn't matter. It's just material stuff, as long as we love each other. Which we do, we did. Did we?

(*She looks at her ring finger*) I don't believe it.

I'm getting ready for my hen party. That's my thing, I'm having everything I want. No compromise. Maybe a year ago I would've wanted a big fancy do, cocktails on the top floor of Sushisamba or something... but you grow up, don't you? Now all that matters is I get to be with my mates. Louise and Tina are both preggers, so we decide to keep it to a daytime at ours. We've got a smart Help to Buy two-bed flat. Enough room for us and a baby. He mentions that a lot. Us and a baby. But we've never discussed kids.

I've laid out all my favourite food. Vol-au-vents with prawns, Mr Kipling's French Fancies, mini sausages with ketchup, loads of crisps, sausage rolls, cheese-and-pineapple-on-sticks in the shape of a big hedgehog, cucumber sandwiches and lots and lots of booze... There's water for the pregnant friends.

I got these gorgeous gold dangly earrings from the girls as an engagement prezzie and I put them on—I want them to see how much I love them. I'm wearing a green plunge-neck pantsuit and I feel brilliant.

Then he comes in, in a grey dressing-gown. His hair is short now, no more floppy bits, but he's somehow found the energy to style it with this paste he gets at £10 a tub from the barbers. It smells like PVA glue. His handsome face is scrunched up with his hangover and it's like the room shrinks to a tunnel.

(*To him, anxious*) Morning darling! (*To audience*) My voice is brittle. (*To him*) Shall I get you some coffee?

She becomes tense and agitated as she pours coffee, and, shaking, walks ever so slowly with the mug towards him.

He likes it strong, with milk—not too much—and one and a half teaspoons of sugar; raw cane; not the white stuff. He likes it in this mug—a present from a work colleague, it has a picture of him smiling on it but the handle is twisted just at the point where you need to grip on to it. It's uncomfortable and impractical, but he likes the way it looks.

(*To him, nervously smiling*) This'll help with the hangover.

I walk through the tunnel. If I am quiet—almost invisible, then he can't get angry. Simple. Just don't do anything to disturb his morning. If he gets his coffee and I leave him alone—(*trails off*)

Her hand shakes, we watch her slow, slow progress from one side of the stage to the other as she wills the mug not to spill.

I'm nearly there, nearly there. And then he goes...

HIM: *(stamping foot)* For fuck's sake, how long does it take to bring me a coffee?

The coffee cup smashes.

WOMAN: Oh God! Oh God!

HIM: Christ.

WOMAN: He chucks a tea towel at me.

She starts mopping and collecting up mug shards.

I risk looking at him. He looks at me like he hates me.

She stands up and goes to put the pieces in the bin.

I realise I've got coffee stains on my knees.

HIM: You're a mess, darling!

WOMAN: I can just get changed...It's not a big deal...

HIM: Maybe it's better that happened, you always say that green thing does nothing for your bingo wings.

WOMAN: I say arms... not bingo wings... and I thought you liked my arms...

He pushes past me and sits next to the table. He grabs a sausage roll. Then another.

HIM: Pass us some ketchup while you're there.

WOMAN: Ah... actually that's meant to be for the hen...

HIM: Oh. That's today, is it? Nice of you to let me know... I'm not really in the mood to have your daft mates in the house.

WOMAN: I feel the tunnel tilt and shift. I'm on unsteady ground.

HIM: Can't you just cancel?

WOMAN: I have to see them—everything's set.

HIM: It's my house too. Don't I get a say? I've got a headache love,

She doesn't know how to respond.

HIM: Don't you want to snuggle with me on the sofa?

WOMAN: I haven't seen my friends for months. You know that.

He laughs and crosses past me to the kitchen. Fills up the kettle, switches it on.

What?

He shrugs.

What? Tell me?

HIM: You haven't seen them for months.

WOMAN: I haven't, I—

HIM: They don't like you.

WOMAN: What?

HIM: They're not your friends.

(*Blending into her own voice, sadly*) Who doesn't see their friends for five months? I thought it was because... but then... Shadé did cancel last minute last time and then... Anna said she'd be free to meet me but only gave me an hour and half window and Su keeps doing that thing where she says 'we must meet up soon—but never actually commits to a specific date... Oh God. Maybe he's right. I thought they liked me.

HIM: (*Suddenly tender*) Sorry babe, but it's obvious, isn't it? They aren't good friends. Certainly not to you. Cancel the party. I bet they weren't gonna show up anyway. Look, you've got me yeah? You've got me...

(*then in her own voice*) you've got me. You don't need them.

I felt—sad, but also—relief—he put his arms around me and it was all OK again. He was being kind, breaking the news gently. Wasn't he?

He's made himself tea in a fresh cup, I open the bin and discard the sharp pieces of his ugly mug. They settle on top of the rotting vegetables. The odour hits me, a bit like food, a bit like death and—it's pulsing, there's something in there... alive, but more happy in decay than in the light, wriggling, morphing, they're clambering over each other, making crisscrossing paths in the darkness, they're everywhere! Agh! They're—oh.

HIM: What now?

WOMAN: Nothing, it's nothing.

HIM: Here, take this.

WOMAN: I hold out my hand and automatically grip. (*Yelps in shock*) He's put a scalding tea bag into my palm. I throw it away and stare at him.

HIM: I didn't think you'd actually take it. God, you are an idiot aren't you?

WOMAN: Before I can figure out how to respond, he takes me in his arms and hugs me tight.

HIM: (*Sweetly*) My little moron.

SCENE FOUR

Pause as we shift back to the present.

WOMAN sees CHLOE, who starts 'talking' to her.

Hey sweetie!

Beat.

Aw really? What happened? Aw love, don't worry, Tracey's like that to everyone, honest. She thinks she's an A-lister, or, maybe she's just afraid of people and hides it really well. Either way, it's not about you.

Beat.

I promise.

Beat.

Yeah. I know. It's tough isn't it?

Beat.

Yeah. I know. You'll get a visiting day soon though, won't you?
(*To audience*) Chloe. Lovely girl. Too trusting, in my opinion.
Cares too much about what people think. Desperate to be
liked. But lovely, lovely. I call her a girl but I think she's a bit
older than me. Got two kids. (*Unsure*) A prohibitive... er .. child
protection plan?... Yeah, she's great. We talk a lot. I dunno.
Feel sorry for her. Bit naive? Reminds me of me, once.

Pause.

You can lose yourself in here. You know when people go on
holiday and they pretend they're someone completely different
from who they were back home? It's like that. People aren't
who they say they are. The difference here is they believe the
fiction. Like Chloe, she talks about how her perfect husband
and kids are going to come on visiting day and then you see
her, every other Saturday, all dressed up, sat opposite three
empty plastic chairs. She always makes an excuse about why
they couldn't make it at the last minute. But they're never
coming. She's not the perfect doting wife and mum. Rumour
is, she tried to kill them.

Do you think some people are better off not being in
relationships? We all want connection, as humans, but it
doesn't mean we are all meant to have partners. Do you think
some people are perfectly happy, perfectly sane—and it's
the relationship that makes them go funny in the head? The
interplay of two people that love each other but also the love
comes from a desire to destroy, somehow? I always felt that,
that there was something deep inside me that he couldn't
understand, and it confused him and made him angry and he
wanted to tear it apart. He tried enough times but he could
never quite get it, never have total power. One of the people in
here said the area in your brain linked to violence is right next
to the one linked to love. Sometimes people get their wires

crossed. The love bleeds across and activates another impulse. They're not responsible for their actions, it's just that their wiring's faulty.

A question.

Is there something you're not telling me? Freddy is... he's OK, isn't he? The bastard hasn't—(*they reassure her*) OK. OK.

A question.

Well, when Freddy was born, it was the biggest, most mind-blowing thing. I knew I was pregnant, I knew what was gonna happen, I've watched enough episodes of 'One Born Every Minute'... but... I didn't really know know that I was going to give birth.

(*Responding to a question*) Well, yeah I knew, (*annoyed*) I just like, wasn't prepared for it. Practically, emotionally.

Another question.

No, not prepared. Life had got... difficult.

Another prompt.

Joy, pure joy. Post-natal elation. I don't know if I've had that feeling before. Or since.

(*Genuine confusion at the question*) He didn't want to come to the birth. He said it was disgusting and, I guess it kind of is, if you're not the one experiencing it. He wouldn't even go down on me, so there was no way he was ever going to—Look. He desperately wanted a son. I just thought, at least that's one thing I can give him. One thing I can do right.

Pause.

I'm starting to feel things again.

She looks reluctant to go on, then hardens her resolve.

I stopped feeling. That's why I'm here. Numbness. Had to step out for a minute, take a ciggie break from the office of existence. Except I've been here six weeks. That's not a cigarette break, that's a sabbatical. That's fucking long-term sick leave. That's concerned phone calls from HR saying (*does an annoying voice*) 'No pressure whatsoever but when are you going to come back or else?'

I could leave here at any time. I just don't want to yet. Better to stay... you agree with me, don't you?

(*Responding to the question*) No. I don't want to go back to the numbness. But what's wrong with staying right where I am? Only a bit forgetful. No, I don't—(*deflecting*)

It's just overwhelming, isn't it? Existing? And I feel so spoiled saying that. But I'm beginning to see, all my decisions up until now, they haven't really been mine at all. They're society or the algorithms or something acting on me. Collecting data and then flooding my synapses with images of what they think I should do.

I'm a people pleaser. Child of divorce, think it's all my fault, desperately trying to get them back together by being nice and quiet and well-behaved. All my life has been about keeping other people happy. Or adhering to some abstract idea of who I should be, fed to me by the world, society, books, fucking Disney. Write that down. No, the Disney part. I probably only got married because all my friends said they wanted to. It's no excuse but my mum wanted grandkids, like, a lot and he really wanted kids and they would like, get together and have these loud, elaborate conversations—My mum adored him, called him 'a beautiful man', he could do no wrong. Ha!—They'd have these talks, in front of me, about how wonderful it would be if I would just hurry up and get pregnant, like I could self-fertilise, like a rare amazonian lizard or a self-propagating flower—and it got under my skin and into my head and in the end it just felt like the path of least resistance, so I caved on that too. It's just what people do, isn't it? You see these images all the time, all those happy little families... I'm a people-pleaser. I did it to please. Got it? Did... it... to... please—

Questioner asks why it's important.

Because that's an important part. Trying to make it all OK when it isn't really.

But when he came, he was so loved. I don't need to explain it to you. If you've felt it you've felt it.

The questioner says they haven't.

Oh right, well no, I don't mean to—it's not like only I as a mother can reach the pinnacle of human experience that is raising a kid, no, no, I just mean that big euphoric love, like the sun is shining inside you. I'm not one of those. I'm not saying it's the exclusive preserve of mothers and represents total fulfilment... It's not a unique feeling. I felt that kind of love the first time I held hands with a boy. I've felt it at work. Even with him, in the early days, his pupils would dilate just looking at me and I'd feel... Shit, I've even felt it watching the sunrise at Glastonbury on MDMA. (*She remembers who she's talking to*) Ah I mean, er, no, forget that, I didn't mean me, that was someone else, telling me... I've heard that drugs can be very nice, but I don't...

Oh, there she goes! Little Miss Swagger. Tilly's an arrogant little—I don't care if she doesn't know any better. So entitled! I never spoke to people like that when I was her age. Or, maybe I did. Hard to remember what it was like being a teenager. It's all a bit misty in my rearview. Oi! Tilly! I want my eyelash curler back, and make sure you clean it! I don't want your skanky Maybelline goop all over it again!

SCENE FIVE

Pause. More questions.

Actually, I'd rather not.

More questions.

Why? What's happened?

They tell her something.

And I'm telling you he is safe.

(*Uncertain*) With my mum.

(*Snaps*) How long have we been doing this?

Pause.

Feels like years.

My card got declined in the Co-op. I said try it again. And again... my cheeks burning with embarrassment. I had to leave my shopping at the till. When I got back to ask him, he just said he needed to move some money out the joint account. But—where is it? He wouldn't say, just said I should trust him, why didn't I trust him?

You know, after you've had it, the Guinea Worm, growing inside you for a year or so, one day, it decides it's taken all it can from you and it plans its exit. It makes a little burning hole in your foot. It's not a quick, sharp exorcism, no! Oh no, you've let it into your life, you can't expect it not to do some damage. You will be in a lot of pain as it wriggles about. It's got big now, this parasite, it fills you. It can take weeks, months to go, while you are there, sprawled out in agony. You're left broken and reeling and thinking; did that actually happen to me? With time, it's surprisingly easy to gloss over and pretend it wasn't that bad. But the damage is done.

It's not a one-time-only thing either. You might imagine that once it happened, you could avoid it happening again. You'd be better at spotting the signs. But no, they can enter your body again and again over a lifetime.

Now I lie awake at night, imagining worms growing in me and larvae exploding out of my body. Yep. That's my mind... and now it's yours too.

Pause.

She chooses to ignore the next question.

The women in here, they're alright, most of them. They're nice people. They're not like real friends though. With your real friends you know they're there for you, even if you don't see them often, you pick up just where you left off. It can be years of silence and then bam! All of that warmth and love is still there and everything that's happened in the meantime washes away. Me and my friends, we all used to joke about being in the old people's home together. You know, how they play old-timey music for old fogeys with dementia? Well, we'd be listening to Backstreet Boys and Spice Girls and all the stuff we loved as kids. Jamming about on our wheelchairs and zimmer frames, having a brilliant time.

I didn't see it. That my friends were gone. It's so incremental. There's the honeymoon period where all your mates give you space anyway because the two of you are spending all your free time banging each other's brains out. But then things get back to normal. At first there's just the odd comment from him, 'Alice called you a boring cow when you were in the loo', or, 'Shadé touched a bit close to my bum when we were all posing for a photo'. You skip a dinner, 'cos he picks a fight just when you're about to go out the door, then it happens again; he flies into a rage just 20 minutes before you're due to leave. Then you're onto him, but his tactics shift and the next time he's saying Freddy's sick, he's just thrown up and it was green. So you stay in. Before you know it, you're not getting invited out any more. You call them up, they don't pick up and they don't ever ring back. Everyone's given up on you.

He was clever about it, I'll give him that. I didn't see what he was doing. I thought it was my choice. Radiators not drains— that's what they say about choosing good friends—except it was looking like all I had around me were drains. It wasn't true, but still, in my head sometimes, I hear his voice. 'They're not good friends, they don't even like you,' and it eats me up inside.

What was my point? Well in here you bond quickly with each other. You bare your souls. You're forced to. But you're all bonded over being a bit, a bit funny. It's just not the same as real friends. And that's good because you don't want to have to stay that way, just to stay friends with them. A lot of people get themselves sorted out in here. It can be the making of you, they say. You don't want a load of loons as mates out there in the real world.

(*Irritated by the question*) Well, I suppose I must be. I'm here, aren't I?

Pause.

He's the reason that I'm here. He is.

Pause as time shifts and she recollects.

SCENE SIX

An important day. Before Fred. We've been dating less than a year. We are going to dinner to meet his younger brother. I drive and he is nagging at my driving the whole way, picking at everything I do. I am relieved when we finally get to Margate. We meet at an Italian restaurant with white tablecloths and I finally relax, because he always behaves well in front of other people. I order wine for us all and after a few sips, I feel warm and comfortable. His brother is nice, asks lots of questions. He's studying psychology and tells us about how they sometimes do experiments on the students. He did this thing with an ice bucket, where all the students in the room have to stick their hands in ice and look at photos. There's another room where they look at the same photos, but no ice. A week later, they all come back and the kids who had their hands in ice remember the photos better. And that experiment is meant to prove that memory is linked to emotion, because sticking your hand in ice creates emotions.

Beat.

Scientists are dumb sometimes. I think it goes the other way. Your mind protects you from bad feelings by letting you forget what happened. It can work like that sometimes, can't it?

Anyway, his brother was really nice. I never met him again.

When we got back to our hotel room, he's suddenly in my face.

HIM: Why did you have to do that?

WOMAN: Sorry? What? What did I do?

HIM: I forgive you, but do you have to show everyone how superior you are, all the time.

WOMAN: I don't understand.

HIM: You didn't even notice? I'm OK with it, but not everyone understands. You can be a little bit too much. You get very—

WOMAN: What? Tell me?

HIM: You made him feel small. It wasn't your place. I know, you get carried away. It was difficult for me to watch you like that.

WOMAN: Like?

HIM: Self-absorbed, oblivious. This dinner was really important. I wish you'd tone it down sometimes. Not be so... you.

WOMAN: (*To audience*) I felt terrible. I knew it was important to him, the first meeting with the only family member he wasn't estranged from. I'd tried my best and yet, I hadn't even noticed that my actions had hurt him.

(*To him*) What did I do? Maybe I can make it up to you?

HIM: You really don't even know? My God! You were insisting on getting the wine menu and tasting the wine, to make him feel... uncultured. Why did you have to taste the wine like that! He is our host. Our host! And you made him feel like shit.

WOMAN: For tasting the wine?

HIM: See! You don't even realise. You have no self-awareness, you just blunder on through life hurting everyone around you and you don't even care. It's like your driving. Reckless! Like a great lumbering giant smashing everything, only thinking about yourself.

WOMAN: (*To audience*) I was shocked. It's hard to accept that about yourself—that you have no sensitivity to other people. It made sense; I was always getting it wrong with him, my friends seemed pissed off with me, but I couldn't work out why... I hadn't even noticed that his brother was uncomfortable, let alone humiliated by what I did... I guess I would need to try harder.

And I did. All I did was try. I kept trying and failing. Trying and failing.

Times shifts.

SCENE SEVEN

He's bored of me. Says I've got fat since Freddy. Annoyed that he was crying all the time. He's teething! He can't help it.

HIM: Take him away, I can't stand it.

WOMAN: I take Freddy in the pushchair and go to visit my mum. Mum?

MOTHER: Come in love. Oh, what's wrong?

WOMAN: I feel like I can't cope!
Mum, it's not... I don't think things are right... I'm worried about Fred...

MOTHER: I'm sure it's not all that bad... it'll all look different soon—he's a decent man-

WOMAN: Why do you keep saying that? Can't you see? He's charming to you but it's all an act! Behind closed doors he's a very different person. He's not nice—

I can't cope anymore. It doesn't feel like it's going to get better. I think I want to go back to work but he says there's no point cos I'll just be working to cover the childcare.

MOTHER: You feel guilty and confused.

WOMAN: Yes, that's it! I do! All the time!

MOTHER: You're so tired you don't know what's real and what's not.

WOMAN: I don't! I'm so tired and confused. I keep panicking. I'm worried about Fred all the time and he doesn't even try to help.

MOTHER: Sounds exactly the same as what I experienced with your dad.

WOMAN: Really?

MOTHER: Every new mother goes through this phase. Of course he can't help you. What can he do? Grow some breasts?!

WOMAN: I don't mean that, I just mean... he tells me I'm doing everything wrong.

MOTHER: Well, you probably are! But don't worry, it's not just you. You're not special, you know. This is all perfectly normal.

WOMAN: Could we maybe stay with you for a bit? Until things calm down? I just... I just need a break, maybe?

MOTHER: You need to work through this together. Face your problems, don't run away from them.

WOMAN: Oh. OK. OK.

I think he hates me. My husband hates me. I can't do anything right and I'm trying so hard, all the time. I remember when it wasn't like this. I remember when things were good between us, and I keep trying to get that back. It's exhausting. I can't. I can't keep going like this. I don't know what it's doing to Freddy, seeing me scared and anxious all the time. And him, he doesn't even want to be in the same room as him. Last night, he even... he raised his hand like he was going to hit him. He told me afterwards he would never actually do it, but... I feel like I'm drowning.

Walking, walking, Freddy in the pram, in the rain, no money to go to a caff. Walking, walking. It's OK, baby, we can go back home at four when Daddy goes out. Out where? Out with who? None of my business, he says. Shouldn't be nosy. At least I might lose some weight. Walking, walking. Raining, raining. A bus. Going fast. Could I...? If I stepped off the pavement at just the right moment. Then... nothing? Better than this. But poor Fred. Can't do that to him. Can't leave him with... Can't live like this either. I need help. Where did my friends go?

I call Jess;

Look Jess, I know you guys don't like me that much any more but—

Pause.

What? My phone never rang.

Pause.

(*Confused*) Hang on. What new number?

You were worried?

(*Suddenly overcome with tears, voice breaking*) Um, sorry Jess, can... can I call you back?'

WOMAN takes the phone from her ear and stares at it.

She inputs her own number into the phone and calls. We hear her voicemail playing back to her. The beep is elongated.

'Hi, me...'

She hangs up and slowly moves the phone away from her ear.

What has he done? All this time, he's been saying they never call 'cos they don't care... but... fuck! I'm not going crazy... He lied...but then... why?

By the time I get home. I'm not sure what to believe. The new reality he's created for me is glitching, but I don't have anything to replace it with. I'm stuck, here in this tiny world, anchored to him by Freddy. There's no way out. Is there?

Pause.

When I see him the next day, I ask about the SIM card—did he switch my number? He says, very gently, that we both got new SIMs six months ago. It was a better plan, or whatever. I've been so tired with getting up in the night to feed Freddy, I've simply forgotten.

It makes sense. Doesn't it?

I text everyone my new number. Jess starts calling once a week. And I try to survive for now.

Pause.

SCENE EIGHT

One year ago. I'm still speaking to Jess on the phone. I don't tell him about it. She's encouraged me to go back to work. He says it's pointless and fights me and fights me, but I won't give in. I need this. So, three days a week, I go.

I go to the office with a thick layer of foundation on, to hide-
... It looks ridiculous like I'm auditioning for 'Love Island'. No-one who works in accounting needs to look like that. I'm scared, all the time—but still hoping it will get better. I post happy pictures of me and little Fred online, face tilted just so.

He gives me 20 quid to spend each week and I get a takeaway coffee every morning. It's not much, but to me, it tastes like independence. Nearly everything I earn goes into paying the nursery to cover the days I'm at work, I understand that. But I do it for the love of it.

I don't think many people love accounting. But I do. There are no grey areas. Either the sum makes sense—it adds up, or it doesn't. There are no conflicts, no arguments, no alternative versions of reality. No wormholes. Just a neat, elegant sum. That's what I do all day. Making things add up. I am good at it. I get it right a lot more often than I get it wrong and while I'm working on the accounts, I don't think about anything else. I am free.

Beat.

One day, my boss tells me I've done a great job, such a great job, I can take the afternoon off. I nearly start crying.

Is everything OK? He asks, shifting awkwardly from one foot to another. You know, my door is always open. We've noticed you've been... less than effervescent lately.

I know, thank you. I think an afternoon off is just what the doctor ordered.

Shaking. I take my bag and my jacket and run for the door. I am dizzy with adrenaline, my heart pounding in my ears, I run onto the street. He thinks I'm at work. He doesn't know where I am, he doesn't know. I click my heels along the pavement in a daze, propelled forward with no certain destination. It's a weird spring day, with a hot sun but cold Atlantic air, the blossom trees are out, pink and fluffy against the blue sky. I'm walking faster now, feeling the pulse of the traffic on the street next to me, the hot-cold of the weather, the firmness of the ground under me. The ancient dignity of the grand old buildings all around. It's all fuel to me, propelling me on, click clack, click clack. I remember with a rush how much I love living in this city and then it hits me with sudden force, I'm alive. I'm still alive! And I can make choices that are my own.

I call Jess. What shall I do?

'Leave,' she says. 'Go, go now. He's at work, right?'

Yes, but Jess, I can't just leave. It's impossible.

JESS: Meet you at your flat.

WOMAN: He promised, just last week, that things are going to be different. He promised me.

JESS: And what happened last time he promised? And the time before that?

WOMAN: It's not about me, but I worry, about Fred...

JESS: I know. You can do this. I'll be with you.

WOMAN: I get home, half-expecting him to be waiting for me, but there's no sign of him. I go to the nursery at the end of the road and I say there's a family emergency and I have to take Freddy out right now. I'm so, so frightened as I walk out of there. I keep thinking about what will happen if he sees me, if he catches me. What will I do? Then, I see Jess. She's all tan and leggy. Just like I remember her. She comes up to me and Freddy and hugs us tight.

'Oh my God, Jess. I can't do this.'

JESS: You can. I'm here.

WOMAN: We walk to the house. Pack a bag for Freddy, a bag for me. Jess gets my passport from the bottom drawer of his desk and we're ready to go. Except. I'm shaking, I'm stuck. I want to move forward, but I can't. It's like worms burning tunnels through my guts.

JESS: It's OK. We can do this. I've got you.

WOMAN: Jess strokes my hair.

I c...c... can't! He'll k...k...k...kill me.

JESS: You can stay with me, at my place. He'll never know you're with me, he doesn't know we still talk, does he?'

WOMAN: N..no... but—

Freddy starts crying. Real, big screams. Even if he does kill me, Jess will protect Freddy. Maybe we can get Freddy out.

My legs move and we hurry to the door. Jess is parked outside. We're just fixing Freddy's car seat, when...

He's there. Walking up the street towards us. Jess sees him too. I am frozen and Freddy is crying, crying, crying.

He walks to the back seat, picks Fred up and takes my hand.

Jess is rambling about going on a trip to the cinema. He simply walks past her and leads us inside the house.

She is cowed and scared.

Things got a lot worse after that.

SCENE NINE

Pause; we return to the present.

WOMAN: Ah... My name? It's there on your form, isn't it?

Well, I dunno. (*Defensive*) I told you, I'm not good with names.
I don't... Tracey? No, that... Chloe? Leslie? Ahhh. Just give me a minute!

Mary, I think it's Mary... But Mary's not meant to be here. She's not meant to be here. He put her here.

One day I went to a work do, which he knew about. He fought me about it, manipulated me, told me I shouldn't go, because they're bad people. We're accountants, we're not exciting enough to be bad, I said. Another punch. Even though I was afraid, I also knew that he would take his anger out on me no matter what I did. So I went.

I was free for a whole evening. I could forget about it all. My Mum was helping look after Fred at the house, until his bedtime. The few hours between Mum leaving and me getting home were a worry, when he'd be alone in the house with my boy... If I thought about it, it made my stomach freeze over. So I danced and drank Malibu and coke to melt the feeling and I felt like a normal person for just a few hours. One of the blokes from IT, Johnny, danced with me. It was weird, feeling different hands on my body. Gentle hands. Shifting to fit the form of another person. He showed me pictures of his dog on his phone, a cute beagle named Lacey. I've always wanted a dog. They just love you, no matter what. Unconditional. You see why people use them as baby replacements. Then he said he'd like to see me without my makeup on. That was weird. I tensed at that. I asked him about working in IT. He said it was a means to an end. His real passion was refurbishing old video game consoles. He had a whole room in his flat dedicated to them. Then we had a debate about which was better, Nintendo or Sega. I played Sonic the Hedgehog non-stop as a kid, he played Super Mario. We both played Mortal Combat and he challenged me to a game. At yours? I said shyly. On the Megadrive?

He said I could pick which character I wanted to play. But then he added, as long as it isn't Johnny Cage, so I guess that's his favourite. I always liked Shang Tsung. He was the shape-shifter.

He was very comfortable to be around. No pretensions. Johnny—not Shang Tsung.

Then he asked if maybe we could go get a Pret together at some point, and I thought about blowing half my week's allowance on one lunch. 'Yeah,' I said. 'OK.'

He offered to wait for my taxi with me but I made some excuse. I didn't want him to see I was getting the bus home.

Pause.

When I opened the front door, there he was, in a chair he'd dragged into the hallway, staring straight ahead, whisky bottle in hand. Eyes rimmed with red.

She shifts into the memory.

I smell stale cigarettes and hear Freddy whimpering in the next room.

He puts the bottle down.

HIM: Apologise, bitch.

WOMAN: I know how this dance goes. I say sorry, I suck his dick, He falls asleep and I lie awake, crying.

I know this dance so well, I don't even think about the steps, I can leave my body to take over and then return to it once the crying part is over.

But then, something snaps. My body won't do the steps. The apology starts to form but withers in my mouth. I look at him, really look at him. His eyes are glazed over, his paunch sticks out and his features have sunk into his face like a landslide. He's just a bag of flesh pretending to be important.

I don't feel scared of him any more, and replacing the fear and the guilt and the self-loathing is this absolute razor-sharp clarity. I will not say sorry to this terrible man. Not tonight. Not ever again.

Not ever.

Not ever.

No, no, no!

Hair pulled

Stairs—up, bang up, bang bang up-stairs. Up! Up! Up! Kidneys, crumble—stairs, bang bang. Slither, burn carpet, slither, can't walk, stumble.

HIM: Say sorry, say sorry!

WOMAN: No - how can I? Why would i-

HIM: Bitch.

WOMAN: Water, bath water

No breath

Lungs burn—panic, burn

(*gasps*) Heart thuds.

HIM: Say sorry.

WOMAN: No.

Lungs burn. Sharp white.

(*Defiant*) No!

Pain. Pain. Thrashing. Dying. Dying. It's not OK. Can't go—

Air.

Dying?

I can't tell.

How dare he?

(*To audience*) That's why, can you see now why?

Black.

Am I still here? I don't know.

Eventually, I find him, still, on the floor. Me, looped over the bath, nose touching water. Exhausted.

It's funny, like some sort of reverse baptism, like my soul's been pulled out of me. I can't feel. He's lying powerless beside me on the sodden bath mat, curled up like a foetus, untroubled by his actions. Without my feelings, it's like I've lost what I had to lose. Suddenly, I am as powerful as him.

I push, intrigued, on the putty of his cheek. He doesn't stir. He's out cold.

I'm so tired, all I want to do is sleep. With no feelings, all I have is my rational mind. It whispers: 'Now's your chance.' I feel I can undo it all. Years of being a good, polite, conventional girl, just trying to make her marriage work. Now I can be whatever I want to be.

I tiptoe downstairs and wrap the whisky glass inside a tea towel and smash it to pieces. I creep back up. His body is so close to the door I only have a crack to squeeze through. I step over him and crouch, right by his face and I whisper:

'One minus zero equals one.'

I scatter the shards of glass around his body and I take the sharpest one. Glistening. I begin my work.

Long pause.

SCENE TEN

It didn't take long for the police to find me.

'Explain to me in detail why you used a piece of glass to carve the words 'STAY AWAY' in capital letters on your husband's forehead?' They said.

'Dunno,' I said.

Pause.

Three doctors agreed I needed to be sectioned. The psychiatric assessment found me in deep need of help. But you know that.

Another question, she chooses to ignore it.

There's this little girl I see around here sometimes, playing outside on the grass or splashing in puddles, or in a corner of the room, sat legs crossed, doing some homework. She wears this knitted red cardigan with yellow tights, a blue top and a pink tutu. Her hair's always tangled. She seems... content. She's got this impish expression, like she's got some special secret plan. She likes maths and hopscotch and vanilla ice cream. She memorises times tables and makes them into songs. She has a bunch of friends at school and even though she's a bit different, they all love her and she loves them. She's got two parents who love her too. All she knows is love and trust. All the sums add up.

Sometimes, out in the garden, she makes mud pies. She can spend hours, just feeling the dirt on her hands, patting and shaping different sculptures from her own imagination. If she sees a worm, she likes to pull it in two, just to see whether there's any truth to that saying that it will grow a new head and crawl away. Fifty-eight dead worms later, she's still testing that theory.

Pause.

Another question.

Why do you keep asking about Fred? Freddy's safe. He's safe. He's somewhere, away from him. I made sure. (I made sure).

She realises something that she had forgotten.

I picture him, in here with me sometimes. He's always safe and warm... sometimes he's a powdery soft newborn and I just—

36

(*she makes a gesture like she's holding him*) powder-soft. Bald. Perfect. Sometimes, he's a toddler, and I see him out the corner of my eye while we're doing group therapy or the relaxation class and he waddles in, chocolate smeared on his face.

She gestures picking him up and swinging him round.

Now, he's sleeping. Sometimes he's playing with the girl, in the mud.

Pause.

I felt this wave come over me—after the—I knew with certainty that when he woke up, if he woke up, he wouldn't just come for me, he'd come for Fred too. I knew even if we ran to the edge of the world he'd find us. He could kill us. He could. After what I'd done to him? He wouldn't stand for it.

Pause.

More questions.

I went to Freddy's room and I wrapped him up in a padded baby-grow. He had this one that made him look like a bear with little ears?

We're going away, baby boy. Far away. Shhh. Shhh. It's OK.

(*Looks at her nails*) There was soil under my nails when they found me.

(*A new recollection returns to her*) I plunged them into the ground. (*Unsure*) Digging for a way out? Making a tunnel. (*Fevered*) A wormhole to another world. The insects rose up and clambered over our hands. So full of rich life. We dug together. We're going to find a way out, Fred. You and me.

It started to rain and the mud slipped between my hands. We had to escape, now or never, now or never. There it was. How come I never saw it before? It had always been there. A wormhole in our back garden. All I had to do was dig. Dig deep and we'd be in our parallel life, the one where I go dancing and I'm not afraid, the one where I wear pantsuits and fly around the world, the one where the sparkle never left my eyes and me and Freddy goes to sleep at night knowing nothing will ever hurt us.

Don't cry baby, it's OK. I won't let anything bad happen ever again. I'm here, shhh, shhh, it's alright, darling. Mummy's with you. Mummy's here.

She shifts from re-enacting what happened to realising what it means. The full impact hits her. She silently screams. After several moments, she recovers enough to speak.

You know how everyone talks about heartbreak? Heart. Break. I felt it. The pain, as my heart cracked in two. Nothing will ever put it back together. That's how it is now. Severed.

And I can't get back to... I want to go back to that first night in the club, surrounded by my friends. I didn't need him. I was complete but I didn't know it. I still had all the power. I had it! And he made that ultimatum. I could have said no then. Not now, not after, but then... I still had a choice. But no-one really has a choice, do they? There are no parallel lives, only this one. We're programmed from the start, to need, to crave, even if it means our own destruction. We spend our lives desiring the thing that will magically fill that yearning within us. I thought he would be that for me. I thought I was that for him.

Pause.

I have to leave now, don't I?

Pause.

Somewhere a tape recorder whirs, clicks and stops recording.

Her mind wanders and resets. The mist descends. She has gone back through the wormhole.

Will Freddy be there? I've really missed him. I miss my baby.

END

ALSO AVAILABLE FROM SALAMANDER STREET

All Salamander Street plays can be bought in bulk at a discount for performance or study. Contact info@salamanderstreet.com to enquire about performance licenses.

TRADE by Ella Dorman-Gajic
ISBN: 9781914228865

Exploring the currency of female bodies in an underground world, Ella Dorman-Gajic's Trade powerfully pulls into question the archetype of the "perfect female victim" by examining the psychology of a morally complex protagonist.

SHE by Anthony Clark
ISBN: 9781739103057

Seven short plays charting the experiences of different women from childhood to old age, these stories, each with an intriguing twist, are visceral, poignant and laced with humour.

ALGORITHMS by Sadie Clark
ISBN: 9781738429394

A bisexual Bridget Jones for the online generation.

these words that'll linger like ghosts till the day i drop down dead by Georgie Bailey
ISBN: 9781914228896

An experimental play about dealing with grief and mental health crises by award-winnning playwright

CLASS by Scotte
ISBN: 9781913630010

Scottee uncovers what it is to be embarrassed about where you're from, how you can pretend to be richer than you are and explores why we all get a thrill from watching how the other half live.

9 781068 696206